ITEM 017 731 875

D1630837

The Home Front

1914-18

UXBRIDGE COLLEGE
LEARNING CENTRE

 MALCOLM CHANDLER

Heinemann Educational Publishers
Halley Court, Jordan Hill, Oxford, OX2 8EJ
a division of Reed Educational & Professional
Publishing Ltd
Heinemann is a registered trademark of Reed
Educational & Professional Publishing Ltd

OXFORD MELBOURNE AUCKLAND
JOHANNESBURG BLANTYRE GABORONE
IBADAN PORTSMOUTH NH (USA) CHICAGO

© Malcolm Chandler 2001

Copyright notice
All rights reserved. No part of this publication may be
reproduced in any material form (including photocopy-
ing or storing it in any medium by electronic means and
whether or not transiently or incidentally to some other
use of this publication) without the prior written permission of the copyright owner, except in accordance with
the provisions of the Copyright, Designs and Patents Act
1988 or under the terms of a licence issued by the
Copyright Licensing Agency Ltd, 90 Tottenham Court
Road, London W1P 0LP. Applications for the copyright
owner's written permission to reproduce any part of this
publication should be addressed to the publisher.

First published 2001

ISBN 0 435 32729 1
04 03 02 01
10 9 8 7 6 5 4 3 2 1

Designed and typeset by Jonathan Williams
Printed and bound in Spain by Edelvives

Photographic acknowledgements
The authors and publisher would like to thank the
following for permission to reproduce photographs:
Hulton Archive: 3A, 20E, 30E; Hulton Getty: 23A;
Imperial War Museum: 7A, 31J; Jeff Moore: 12A; Mary
Evans Picture Library: 18B; Punch: 5A; Robert Hunt
Library: 14A.
Cover photograph: © Hulton Getty
Picture research by Liz Moore

The Home Front 1914–18

Contents

'The great emotion was excitement'

On 4 August 1914, Britain declared war on Germany. The popular reaction to the war was one of great enthusiasm. Looking back it is hard to imagine that anybody could have been so enthusiastic about the outbreak of a war, but in August 1914 very few people had any idea of what lay in store for them. Much more important was what had been happening in the last few years before the outbreak of war. These years had been very difficult for Britain.

Syndicalism

Discontent with working conditions led to a wave of strikes that affected Britain from 1908. These were organised by a new and aggressive form of trade unionism called syndicalism. Some trade unions believed that a general strike, with workers from a number of different unions putting pressure on the government, was the best way to bring about political and social change. The strikes led to violent clashes between strikers and the police and the army, who were used in an effort to keep order, and a number of demonstrators were killed. As a result, three unions – the transport workers, the coalminers and the railwaymen – formed the Triple Alliance and planned a general strike for September 1914. But when the war broke out, the strike was called off.

Anarchism

Alongside syndicalism, there was also a series of anarchist demonstrations in the years leading up to the war. Anarchists are people who are opposed to all laws and all governments.

SOURCE A

▲ **Crowds demonstrating as meat vans leave the docks for market during the 1912 transport workers' strike.**

Suffragettes

During the period 1905 to 1914 there had been growing agitation by the Suffragettes, who campaigned for Votes for Women. When the Women's Social and Political Union (WSPU) was set up in 1903, it was a non-violent organisation. However, after the general election of 1906, the Suffragettes (as members of the WSPU became known) began a campaign to try to force the government to give women the vote. At first they simply heckled politicians and tried to disrupt meetings, but by 1912 they were setting fire to factories and churches and carrying out repeated acts of sabotage and vandalism. Cabinet ministers were hounded and attacked whenever they appeared in public.

When war broke out the leader of the Suffragettes, Emmeline Pankhurst, called off the campaign and urged her followers to support the war effort. But Christabel, Emmeline Pankhurst's second daughter, continued to edit the movement's newspaper, *The Suffragette*. She also encouraged women to play a more active role in the war effort, organising the 'Right to Serve' campaign in 1915 (see page 18).

Ireland

By far the most serious sequence of events in the years leading up to the outbreak of war in August 1914 took place in Ireland, which at that time was entirely governed by Britain. In 1912 the Liberal government had introduced a Home Rule Bill into Parliament. This was aimed at giving Ireland self-government, but the Bill was defeated in the House of Lords. This meant that the Bill could not become law for another two years.

The Protestants in Ulster were strongly opposed to Home Rule because they wanted Ireland to remain united with Great Britain. In an independent Ireland there would be more Catholics than Protestants. The Protestants were afraid that the Catholics would outvote them and force changes in education and worship, even take away some of their rights to free speech. They also thought that the Catholics would perhaps cut the links between Ireland and the rest of Britain that they cherished.

From 1912 to 1914 the situation in Ireland became more and more dangerous. The Ulster Volunteers were set up to defend the Protestants, and by 1914 numbered 450,000. They bought arms from abroad and smuggled them into Ireland. In retaliation, the Dublin Volunteers were set up by Catholics and they too collected arms. By 1914 it was estimated that there were about 600,000 armed men in Ireland.

In March 1914 British officers stationed at the Curragh, a military base near Dublin, stated that they would not try to force Home Rule on Ulster, even if they were ordered to do so. This incident came to be known as the Curragh Mutiny and it suggested that the situation in Ireland was now very serious indeed. It seemed that a civil war was about to break out between North and South, between Catholics and Protestants, and that the British government would be unable to rely on its own troops to act in an emergency.

In the summer of 1914 the crisis was so serious that King George V called a conference at Westminster to try to sort out the problems. It met from 21 to 26 July 1914. The Westminster Conference coincided with the climax of a crisis elsewhere in Europe. On 28 June the Archduke Franz Ferdinand, the heir to the Austrian throne, had been assassinated by Serbs in Sarajevo. The Austrian government finally delivered an ultimatum to Serbia on 23 July and the Serbs in turn rejected it on 25 July. The Westminster Conference meant that public attention in Britain was not focused on what was happening in Europe. However, when war broke out just over a week later, the crisis in Ireland simply disappeared and many Irishmen volunteered for the British army. In fact, during the years from 1914 to 1918 at least 100,000 men from Ireland served in the British armed forces.

When war broke out in 1914 a number of internal conflicts in Britain were put on hold. None of them actually disappeared – all returned either during or after the war.

But for the time being the British people could concentrate their efforts and emotions on defeating a foreign enemy.

The outbreak of war

When Britain went to war on 4 August 1914 in many ways it came as no surprise. For some time there had been suggestions of a possible war with Germany. The German Kaiser's actions in Morocco in 1905 and 1911 had been attacked in the British press and he had been accused of being aggressive, arrogant and overbearing. The Second Morocco Crisis in 1911 resulted in a threatening speech by the British Chancellor of the Exchequer, David Lloyd George. He warned the German government not to interfere in matters that did not concern it and threatened action.

Britain had not been directly involved in the events of late July and the first few days of August 1914. When the Austrian ultimatum to Serbia was rejected on 25 July (see page 4), Austria declared war against Serbia. This declaration resulted in Russia declaring its support for Serbia, and Germany declaring its support for Austria. The German government expected that France would declare war in support of Russia and so began the Schlieffen Plan. This was an attempt to knock out Russia's main ally by advancing through Belgium. Under the 1839 Treaty of Westminster, Britain was committed to defend Belgium if it was attacked, and so the British government declared war on Germany on 4 August 1914.

In Britain, it was relatively easy to whip up hatred of Germany and the Germans, and this took place in the days after the declaration of war. Newspapers printed stories calling on Britain to 'stand by Belgium'. A famous cartoon showed a small boy stopping a huge bully in his tracks (see Source A).

British troops were sent to Belgium as quickly as possible in August 1914. London buses were taken over the Channel to carry troops to the front-line. The British Press took up the themes of Belgian heroism and German barbarity and there were incredible stories published about the atrocities being carried out by German troops. One newspaper report described German soldiers running amok through a Belgian maternity hospital, spearing new-born babies on their bayonets.

SOURCE A

BRAVO, BELGIUM!

▲ A British cartoon published in August 1914 which shows Belgium being bullied by Germany.

Even more unlikely was a story that was published in several countries in August 1914 describing the behaviour of German troops in Antwerp. The story began in a German newspaper after Antwerp was captured by the Germans and was then added to by newspapers all over Europe. Here are four of the newspaper stories, including the original German version.

 SOURCE B

When the fall of Antwerp became known, the church bells were rung in Cologne.

Extract from the German newspaper, *Kölnische Zeitung*.

 SOURCE C

According to the Kölnische Zeitung, *the clergy of Antwerp were compelled to ring the church bells when the fortress was taken.*

Extract from the French newspaper, *Le Matin*.

 **SOURCE D**

According to what The Times *has heard from Cologne via Paris, the unfortunate Belgian priests who refused to ring the church bells when Antwerp was taken have been sentenced to hard labour.*

Extract from the Italian newspaper, *Corriere della Sera*.

 SOURCE E

According to information which has reached the Corriere della Sera *from Cologne via London, it is confirmed that the barbaric German conquerors of Antwerp punished the unfortunate Belgian priests for their heroic refusal to ring the church bells by hanging them as living clappers to the bells with their heads down.*

Extract from *Le Matin*.

Government intervention

The stories that appeared in the press in the early months of the war had the desired effect on the British public. German goods were boycotted or thrown away. An advertisement in The Times *asked its readers to demand to see the passports of waiters if their accents sounded German. One elderly lady decided to act without waiting for proof of nationality and tipped her soup over a waiter who sounded German. He then produced his passport, which proved that he was Swiss.*

This wave of anti-German hysteria suited the government – they wanted the British public to support the war against Germany and her allies. Herbert Asquith, the prime minister, intended to reassure the British people that their lives were not going to be greatly affected by what was happening on the continent. Like almost everybody else in Britain, and indeed across Europe, Asquith expected that the war would be over quickly. So he adopted the slogan 'business as usual' to suggest that the war could be fought without disturbing life in Britain. He followed this up with the slogan 'over by Christmas', which suggested that all the fighting would be over within a few months and, of course, that Britain would be successful.

To reassure the British people even further, Asquith appointed Field Marshal Kitchener to run the war. Kitchener was a national hero, whose experiences abroad were many and included great military success in the Sudan, in the Boer War in South Africa, and in the reorganisation of military forces in India. He inspired the confidence of the British people. On the most famous of all recruiting posters, all that was necessary was to put Kitchener's face with a finger pointing at anybody passing (see Source A). There was no name on the poster, because Kitchener was instantly recognisable.

From August 1914 Kitchener was in charge of overall strategy, recruitment and training, and supplies. It was an impossible task and one that became increasingly difficult the longer the war lasted. In fact, Kitchener was one of the few military leaders to believe that the war would not be over quickly, but he could not have expected the fighting to be so horrific.

After the initial propaganda campaign against the Germans, propaganda became more subtle. Posters continued to be the main method used by the government to publicise

SOURCE A

BRITONS

"WANTS
YOU"

JOIN YOUR COUNTRY'S ARMY!
GOD SAVE THE KING

▲ A British army recruitment poster of 1914. Kitchener points the finger.

so-called German atrocities. Some, such as the Great Body Scandal, were completely false. This was a story published in 1917 which stated that the Germans collected the dead bodies of British soldiers and turned them into fat (it was not officially denied until 1925). Other stories, like the shelling of Scarborough and Hartlepool, the sinking of the Lusitania and the execution of Nurse Edith Cavell, were true.

The shelling of Hartlepool and Scarborough by German ships occurred in December 1914. 119 people, including babies and children, were killed in Hartlepool alone. The raids led to fear of a German invasion, but they also united the British people against the Germans. The government made full use of this in its recruiting campaign (see Source B).

The British passenger liner the Lusitania sank in 1915 after being struck by a single torpedo from a German submarine. The Germans gave no warning of the attack and over 1000 passengers drowned. Britain again made the most of this event in the propaganda war, portraying the Germans as murderers of innocent people.

Edith Cavell was an English nurse who became matron of a Red Cross hospital in Belgium during the war. Edith nursed thousands of wounded Allied soldiers who had been captured by the Germans, but she also helped hundreds to escape. When she was discovered by the Germans she was arrested as a spy and sentenced to death. Countries around the world pleaded for her to be spared, but she was executed by firing squad in 1915. Edith became a national heroine and her story was used in propaganda campaigns, to show how evil the Germans were and that British women were capable of great courage.

From 1915 the government made films to encourage support for the war effort, and in 1916 the film Battle of the Somme was shown

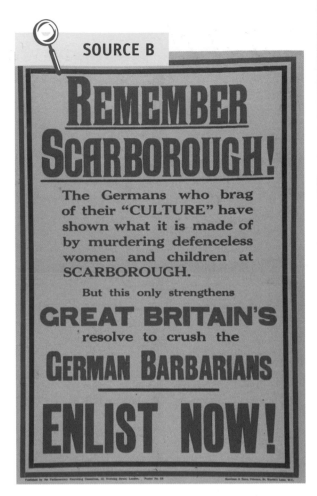

▲ **A recruiting poster produced after the German naval bombing of Scarborough.**

in cinemas all over Britain. It was watched by more than 20 million people. The film did not show any actual fighting and mostly concentrated on the build up to the battle. Unfortunately for the government, the film did not have the desired effect. Instead of encouraging support for the war, it actually produced anti-war feelings, because it showed pictures of wounded British soldiers.

In 1917 the Ministry of Information was set up to censor information and produce films. These were usually short films encouraging women to volunteer for work in munitions factories. The National War Aims Committee was also set up. It published leaflets and held rallies to keep up morale.

The Defence of the Realm Act, 1914

In August 1914 the government passed the Defence of the Realm Act (DORA). This gave the government extensive powers to protect Britain from invasion and to take effective actions to win the war.

The Defence of the Realm Act introduced censorship on all matters concerned with the war: newspapers were censored and it was forbidden to discuss the war in a public place. The law was changed so that suspected spies could be held without trial. Restrictions were made on the right of trade unions to strike and to bargain for increased pay. The government also had the power to control rents and prices, and to take over factories and land for war production. The government also introduced restrictions on hoarding food and profiteering. These were attempts to prevent people from taking advantage of shortages of food by forcing up prices.

 SOURCE A

It is without doubt largely due to drink that we are unable to secure the output of war material needed to meet the requirements of the Army.

The King will set the example by giving up all alcoholic liquor himself, and issuing orders against its consumption in the Royal Household, so that no difference shall be made between the treatment of rich and poor.

A statement issued by King George V in August 1914.

British Summer Time was introduced in 1916. This was intended to increase the hours available for work: an extra hour of daylight in the evening meant people in factories could work longer. To cut down on drunkenness and to try to ensure that workers arrived on time for work, the opening hours of public houses were limited. Alcoholic drinks were watered down and buying rounds of drinks was banned. Even King George V did his part to discourage the drinking of alcohol (see Source A). During the war, convictions for drunkenness fell from 3388 in 1914, to 449 in 1918.

The impact of war on the British people

During the First World War the British people found themselves much closer to war than ever before. This was especially so in December 1914 when German warships bombarded ports along the east coast, including Hartlepool and Scarborough where nineteen people were killed. There was also the threat from the air: in the 106 air-raids in Britain from 1915 to 1918 about 1400 people were killed.

From January 1915 Zeppelins began to make bombing raids on British cities. Zeppelins were airships filled with hydrogen (see Source B on page 10) that could fly at 4600 metres (15,000 feet). British fighters in 1915 could only fly at 13,000 feet, and so could not attack the Zeppelins. Altogether there were 51 Zeppelin raids in 1915 and 1916, but they stopped in 1917 because of improved British defences. These included the use of searchlights, which meant that the Zeppelins could be easily spotted and fired at. If a Zeppelin was hit it burst into flames and the crew had little chance of surviving. The first

▲ A Zeppelin airship.

Zeppelin to be shot down was at Cuffley in Hertfordshire in October 1916. The successful pilot was awarded the Victoria Cross. In total, about 500 civilians died as a result of Zeppelin raids.

From May 1917 the Germans began air-raids using aeroplanes known as Gotha IV bombers. These continued to the end of the war, by which time there had been 57 raids. The damage caused in air-raids was small compared to that during the Second World War: the bombs used weighed only about 100 kilograms and usually destroyed no more than a few houses at most. The effect of the raids, however, was dramatic, as nothing like this had ever happened in Britain before. The loss of life was also high, as there were few ways that people could protect themselves. In June 1917, 20 Gothas carried out a bombing raid on London in which 162 civilians were killed and 432 injured. In total, over 850 people were killed in Gotha raids on Britain during the First World War.

As the war progressed people in Britain began to suffer from food shortages. The most serious ones began in 1916, when the Germans started unrestricted U-boat (submarine) warfare. This meant that ships carrying goods to Britain were sunk without warning. Rationing was introduced (see page 25), but there was little real hardship.

Recruitment

The British army in August 1914 was a professional army. This meant it was manned entirely by volunteers who were highly trained. By most European standards it was tiny, about 350,000 men, which led to the Kaiser describing it as a 'contemptible little army'. Because Asquith was determined to maintain the idea of 'business as usual', the policy of recruiting men to the army as volunteers continued. In August 1914 the introduction of conscription (compulsory military service) would have been unthinkable. It would have created fears of a prolonged war, and of disruption of everyday life. In fact Kitchener was quite happy to rely on volunteers. Not only did he believe that it would be possible to raise enough recruits in this manner, but he also believed that volunteers would fight more effectively than conscripts.

The government acted quickly to recruit volunteers to fight. On 6 August 1914 Parliament agreed to increase the army to 500,000. The famous Kitchener poster (see Source A on page 7) appeared on 7 August and recruiting offices were immediately besieged. By the end of August 300,000 men had volunteered. In September another 600,000 men were called for and 450,000 more had volunteered by the end of the month. By December an army of 4 million was planned. But while hundreds of thousands of men volunteered, recruitment was not as successful as the government would have liked.

There were two broad categories of recruits. Many men volunteered out of a sense of honour and were then often the first to be killed as attacks advanced across 'No Man's Land' – the area between the German and Allied lines. They were the 'lost generation', as they became known after the war.

More numerous were recruits who volunteered because they were unemployed. Unemployment figures had been rising in Britain for several years prior to 1914, and where unemployment was worst, recruitment was most successful.

How was recruitment carried out?

The first and most straightforward method of recruitment was by propaganda posters, which in August and September 1914 were usually very simple and did no more than ask men to come forward. Other methods included appeals made at football matches, or by actresses who interrupted performances in music halls to call for men to come onto the stage and join up.

Men who volunteered were grouped into units according to the area from which they came. The idea was a good one in theory. It meant that volunteers were surrounded by friends and acquaintances, but in practice this proved to be a dreadful mistake. 'Pals Battalions', as these local units came to be called, were very effective in enabling new recruits to settle into army life, but had dreadful unforeseen consequences. When a Pals Battalion went into action, particularly if it was on the first day of a major battle, it could suffer very heavy casualties. For example, on the first morning of the Battle of the Somme, units that were ordered to charge on enemy trenches – to go 'over the top' – had 70 per cent of their men killed or seriously wounded. This meant that local areas in Britain could lose a large proportion of their young men in a very short space of time (see Source A on page 12).

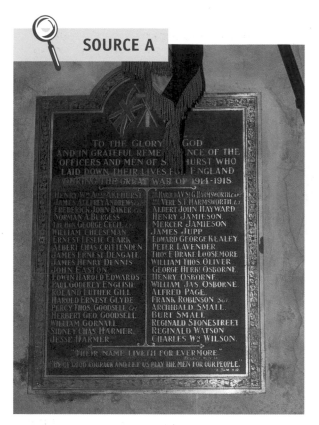

▲ This village war memorial reflects the tragic loss of life that was experienced by local communities.

Recruitment in 1915

By December 1914 the number of volunteers had fallen to 117,000 a month, and by February 1915 to 88,000 a month. The war was not over by Christmas. News of the conditions at the front, and of the high number of casualties, was reaching Britain. At first newspapers printed lists of those killed and wounded, but as numbers grew the government banned all such lists. Newspapers reacted by leaving blank spaces where the lists would have been. Volunteering became less attractive. Many early volunteers had come from the unemployed, but as the war became more and more serious, unemployment fell and wages rose, so men preferred to stay at home rather than take their chance in the army for low pay.

By early 1915 recruitment posters were beginning to become more direct. They carried slogans such as 'Daddy, what did you do in the Great War?' (see Source B). This implied that fathers would be faced with awkward questions if they did not volunteer. The government also tried to use women to put pressure on their husbands, brothers and sweethearts: 'Women of Britain say Go' was one slogan used. Able-bodied men who did not volunteer were seen as cowards. Women approached young men who had not volunteered, usually in very public places, and handed them white feathers (a sign of cowardice).

In August 1915 the national registration of all single men was introduced; later this was extended to all married men. This register compiled a list of all men who had not yet volunteered and who could be called upon to fight if necessary. But before national

Daddy, what did *YOU* do in the Great War?

▲ A recruiting poster produced by the government in 1915.

registration took place, one final effort was made to persuade volunteers to come forward and Lord Derby organised a massive recruitment campaign in late 1915. The campaign failed to encourage enough men to volunteer.

By December 1915 some 2.5 million men had volunteered since the beginning of the war, but to meet the demands of the army, conscription was introduced the following year.

 # Conscription

Conscription means compulsory military service and it was introduced in Britain for the first time by the Military Service Act of January 1916.

General Haig, who became the British commander-in-chief in December 1915, believed in the 'big push'. He was certain that the war could only be won by breaking through the enemy lines on the Western Front, so he demanded that more and more men be sent to France. From 1916 to 1918 some 3,500,000 men were conscripted into the armed forces.

The Military Service Act

The Military Service Act made all unmarried men between the ages of 18 and 41 liable for service in the armed forces. In May 1916 the Act was extended to include married men.

Conscripts could claim exemption on any one of four grounds:

- Ill health.

- Reserved occupation. This meant that they were employed in an industry of national importance, such as mining.

- Family responsibility. This meant that they had dependants who would suffer if they were conscripted.

- Conscientious objection. Men who objected to the war on moral grounds.

What happened if a man claimed exemption?

Anyone who claimed exemption had to go before a Military Tribunal and prove that they deserved to be exempt from military service. The tribunals could reach any one of four decisions:

- Absolute exemption. This meant that the individual was declared unconditionally exempt from service.

- Conditional exemption. This meant that the individual was exempted providing that he undertook work of national importance.

- Exemption from combatant duties. This meant that the individual had to join the armed forces but would not be required to be part of a fighting unit. This usually entailed joining something like an ambulance unit.

- Rejection. This meant that the individual had to join the army and was subject to normal military discipline.

The Military Service Act produced two groups of conscientious objectors. Non-combatants, whose beliefs prevented them from fighting but who were prepared to enlist and accept army discipline, and absolutists, who refused to do any form of military service.

▲ Conscientious objectors serving sentences of hard labour at a Scottish quarry.

What happened to conscientious objectors?

Some 16,000 men were non-combatants. They joined the army and performed duties such as those of medical orderlies, drivers and stretcher bearers.

Some 1500 men were absolutists. They refused to accept any form of military discipline, and would not join the army, wear uniform or follow any orders.

Absolutists could be ordered to join the army. If they refused to obey orders they could be court-martialled and even shot. They could also be sent to prison where they would be forced to do hard labour. During the war, ten conscientious objectors died in prison and another twenty died soon after their release, as a result of the conditions they were forced to endure.

From June 1916 conscientious objectors (COs or conchies, as they became known) were sent to Home Office Work Centres. At the centre in Dyce near Aberdeen, conditions were so cold and harsh (tents were the only accommodation provided) that pneumonia broke out and several men died. At Broxbourne in Hertfordshire, the CO's usual job was handling the rotting corpses of animals. At Princetown on Dartmoor, COs broke rocks or stitched mailbags.

Although conditions in the Home Office Work Centres improved after 1916, they were not closed until April 1919, six months after the war ended. By that time 73 conscientious objectors had died as a result of their treatment in Home Office Work Centres, and another 31 had been driven insane.

The changing role and status of women

In 1914 at the outbreak of the First World War, nearly 5.9 million women were working in Britain out of a total female population of 23.7 million. The most common job was domestic service and about 1.5 million women worked as domestic servants. About 900,000 women worked in textiles and another 500,000 in the 'sweated trades' – the term for work involving low pay, excessive hours of work and insanitary conditions. Women were normally paid two-thirds of a man's wage, or even less, and were rarely promoted above men.

Domestic service

Some domestic servants worked in very bad conditions. They lived in the attics of houses and worked long hours as cleaners, cooks or chambermaids. Their pay was very low, sometimes only £5 or £10 per year, and they often only got one half day a week – or even a month – off. Servants who 'lived out' (in their own homes) were better paid.

Domestic service attracted many young women because the school leaving age was twelve, so many went straight into service. Pay was very low because there were many girls looking for work and it was a job that did not require a high level of education. Most of the work was manual.

Textiles

The textiles industry was a major employer of women, as it had been since the Industrial Revolution. Women could supervise the spinning and weaving machines as effectively as men, but men filled most of the posts of overseers. In the textiles industry pay for women was much lower than for men.

SOURCE A

When I was about fourteen years of age I went to service for about eighteen months. I did not like it at all because you was on from morning to night, and you never did know when you was done, and you never did get your meals in peace for you are up and down all the time. You only get half a day off a week and you never get very large wages in service.

Description of domestic service written in 1906.

SOURCE B

Being in a mill was like being in a prison, and it had the further disadvantage that one was being slowly melted away. In my first two years my weight remained the same, although I grew a couple of inches. Most of us developed speed, but we lacked weight and strength – the work made us human whippets. One day was like another. It was throb, throb, throb.

A description of working in a textile factory just before the First World War. This shows how demanding the work could be.

The sweated trades

The sweated trades also employed large numbers of women, possibly as many as 950,000. The worst examples of the sweated industries were clothing and dressmaking, where women worked in workshops in the houses of their employers. Conditions could be dreadful and the pay very low. Some women worked at home and were paid piece rates (in other words they were paid for each piece they produced). They made goods like jewellery, or painted lead soldiers.

Women were an easy target for the owners of sweatshops. The workers could not afford to complain or they would lose their jobs, and it was almost impossible to set up trade unions because the numbers in each workshop were so small.

Generally, it was not difficult for women to get work, but they usually had to put up with the worst conditions and the lowest pay, often about two-thirds of a man's, or even less.

Women's education

It was very difficult for women to be promoted. Many people simply thought that women were less capable than men. One reason for this was that women were often not as well educated as men. Before 1876 education had not been compulsory and it was not free until 1880. Some families educated their sons, but not their daughters, because it was assumed that women would get married and have children.

In 1902 the school leaving age was raised to twelve, but this only extended elementary (primary) education for a further two years. Staying at school after the age of twelve either meant paying school fees or winning a scholarship. Once again, parents would sometimes pay for a son, but not for a daughter. Even if a girl won a scholarship, parents would often refuse to allow her to take it up because they would lose her earnings. As a result, only 10 per cent of children attended school after the age of

▲ Average pay rates per hour for men and women in 1906.

twelve, and only 10 per cent of those children were girls. This meant that only about 2 per cent of girls received secondary education. It was difficult for women to do much to change the situation: they had fewer rights than men and could not vote. There were also no laws to protect women against discrimination.

Women in the professions

There were, by 1914, women working in almost all the professions. Women had been able to become doctors since the 1870s and could qualify for degrees at some universities. However, there was considerable resistance to their employment. The First World War was to provide the first real opportunity for career development for many highly qualified women.

The impact of war on women

During the First World War more than 6 million British people joined the armed forces. This left many jobs to be filled at home, and as a result about 1.2 million women went to work for the first time. Many women had always worked, but many middle-class women had never worked before. But these changes did not happen immediately.

Some women wanted to play a more active role in the war effort. One group, led by Dr Elsie Inglis, volunteered to go to France and work as nurses, but they were turned down by the War Office with the reply, 'My good lady, go home and sit still'. Elsie Inglis's response was to go home and set up her own organisation, the Scottish Women's Hospital. Within months she and her helpers were working in France, despite the War Office.

A similar refusal was given to members of the First Aid Nursing Yeomanry, which had been set up in 1907. They called themselves the 'First Anywheres', but eventually became known as FANY. In 1914, offers of help from FANY were turned down by the government, as part of Asquith's 'business as usual' policy. Recruiting large numbers of women would have suggested that the war was not going to be over quickly.

Women at the Front

Some women simply ignored the War Office's advice and went to the Front regardless. They formed their own organisations, such as the Women's Hospital Corps (WHS), which was made up of doctors and surgeons, and the Women's Emergency Corps (WES), which provided despatch riders. By October 1914 there were many women working alongside the British Expeditionary Force in Ypres. Source A describes members of the WES.

Though it was obvious by 1915 that the war was not going to be over quickly, the government clung to its policy of 'business as

SOURCE A

It is a queer side of the war to see young, pretty English girls in khaki and thick boots, coming in from the trenches, where they have been picking up wounded men within a hundred yards of the enemy's lines and carrying them away on stretchers.

An extract from the diary of an officer serving in the British Expeditionary Force at Ypres in Belgium, 12 October 1914.

▲ **Women campaigning in 1915 to be part of the war effort.**

usual'. In the spring of 1915, Herbert Asquith, the prime minister, went on a speaking tour of Britain to talk to the 'Workers of Industry'. This was an attempt to boost morale on the Home Front as the war dragged on into its second year. Entry to Asquith's meetings was free, but by ticket only. Printed clearly on every ticket were the words, 'This meeting is for men only'. The significance of the words was obvious: women were not considered to be part of the war effort.

Women in munitions factories

The event that brought women into the war effort in large numbers was the Great Shell Shortage of May 1915. Supplies of ammunition for troops on the Western Front

fell so low that they were unable to fire their guns. David Lloyd George became Minister for Munitions and at once began attempts to increase the production of weapons and ammunition. This meant that many more workers were needed, and the obvious answer was to employ women.

Lloyd George's efforts to expand the industry coincided with the 'Right to Work' March organised by the Suffragettes in London in July 1915, in which 30,000 women took part. Since 1903 the Suffragettes had been campaigning for women to be able to vote. Their slogan was 'the right to vote', but it changed to 'the right to serve' with the outbreak of the war, showing their commitment to the war effort.

SOURCE C

As soon as I heard about the call for women to register for war work I shot down to Camden Town Labour Exchange. When nothing happened I found myself a job at a factory in Grays Inn Road. It was only a small place, with white-washed walls and stone floors. The factory made fuses for shells and apart from the tool-makers and the foremen all the staff were female. It was a twenty-four hour operation with three eight-hour shifts working on a six-week cycle. We women were paid 5½d (2p) per hour, but the men tool-makers got 2/6d (12p). If our work was up to scratch, every six weeks, when we changed shifts, we received a bonus. We had caps to cover our hair, and to stop the hot brass hitting our necks we turned our collars up, but otherwise we had no protection. There were minor accidents, of course, but I don't remember any serious ones.

A munitions worker recalls her work during the First World War.

The shell shortage also brought an end to 'business as usual'. Asquith, a Liberal, agreed to set up a coalition government, with Conservative and Labour members (see page 24). This was a clear sign that the war could not be won without reorganising the nation.

By the end of 1915, 2.5 million men had volunteered for service in the army. An army of that size needed vast supplies of munitions, and more and more women were needed to supply them. Women took the places in munitions factories of the men who fought abroad. They also worked in new factories that opened to produce planes, weapons and ammunition. A National Register was set up to collect the names of women who were ready to take on war work. For many women, this was the start of a new life (see Source C).

The work in the new munitions factories could be very dangerous and unpleasant. Women would catch lung diseases and explosive powder made the skin turn yellow. As a result, some women were nicknamed 'canaries', or 'munitionettes'. Safety precautions were only basic and many women inhaled poisonous chemicals. As a result, some women became unable to have children.

Despite the risks, hundreds of thousands of women worked in munitions factories for the relatively high wages the work received: £3 a week. Many women gave up their jobs as domestic servants for the freedom that came with the wages. By the end of the war over 900,000 women were employed in munitions factories.

The employment of women was not always popular. In 1915 there were strikes against women workers and the government was forced to sign agreements with unions which stated that women would not keep their jobs at the end of the war. One complaint of male workers was against 'dilution'. They were afraid that the employment of unskilled women would lead to lower wages because the women would be doing the same work as skilled men. In some factories notices were displayed warning women that they would be dismissed when the war came to an end.

Male workers showed their disapproval by refusing to help women workers. They also played practical jokes on them, or gave them confusing instructions.

Women in other occupations

Munitions factories were not the only places in which women found work in 1915. Women joined the police force (see Source D) and they also began working in the Land Army, where they took the places of male farm-workers. Land girls, as they became known, began to wear trousers, which became acceptable in public for the first time. By working on the land these women helped to ensure that the country was supplied with food. Altogether about 13,000 women volunteered to work on the land.

By the end of 1915 the significance of women's war work was recognised by many. A new publication, *The Home Service Corps Review,* was set up to describe the contribution of workers on what became known as the Home Front. It published articles about war work, but also printed letters from women who had volunteered (see Source F on page 21).

(see Source F on page 21)

SOURCE D

London has not yet grown accustomed to its policewomen. I saw one today at the corner of Whitehall, and she appeared conscious of the attention she was attracting. Physically the women are not of the type you would expect and they seem little fitted to face the hurly-burly of a street fight. If the women act with tact and discretion, there is useful work for them to do in the quieter parts of the West End of London, but the average East End Cockney seems at present to resent their presence on the streets.

A report from the *Sussex Times* of May 1915 which describes public reactions to women members of the police force.

SOURCE E

▲ **Land girls on a farm in Surrey, April 1917.**

SOURCE F

I have been here a fortnight today, and got my uniform the day before I came. I am learning all kinds of outdoor work, and can milk, feed calves and pigs and poultry, and drive the milk float. I get up at four every morning and enter the joys of milking. I was knocked over by a calf this morning and my hand is pretty badly hurt.

My farmer is also the village blacksmith, and I am learning to shoe a horse and blow the bellows. Some people tell me that I shall not be able to go on with my farm work in the winter, but I intend to stick to it. Our men don't stop fighting in the cold weather, and neither shall I. My only brother is in the trenches – so you know how I feel about it.

An extract from *The Home Service Corps Review,* in 1915.

In 1916, after the passing of the Military Service Acts, the need for women workers became even greater as men were now conscripted into the army. The government finally realised the importance of the contribution that women could make to the war effort and they began to enter many occupations.

The number of women working in industry rose quickly, as did the number of different types of work undertaken by women. By 1917, one third of all women in employment had replaced a man since the beginning of the war. In the same year, the government published a list of all the processes and occupations that women had taken over since 1914, which included brickmakers, tram and bus drivers, conductresses, welders, ticket inspectors, carpenters, porters, van drivers, theatre managers, electricians and foresters.

Two industries that expanded very rapidly during the war were motor car manufacturing and aeroplane construction. Both made use of large numbers of female recruits. Women began to work as car mechanics or drivers and also found work in the aeroplane industry, for example painting the canvas covering of planes with varnish (which was dangerous work as the fumes were poisonous).

Women in the professions

The massive losses incurred by the army on the Western Front destroyed any reluctance to use women in the medical professions. In 1914, Sir Frederick Treves, a famous surgeon, stated that there was no work suitable for women in the sphere of war. By 1917 there were hundreds of women doctors and thousands of nurses treating wounded servicemen both in France and Britain.

Women also began to be accepted into the professions. Many women had worked as primary school teachers before 1914, but by 1919 they occupied more than half of all posts. Women also began to be accepted in the legal professions. In 1916 banks began to use women to collect money from branches in the city, and Reuters, the news agency, used women as messengers. In 1917 the first woman diplomat was appointed by the British government.

Women in the armed forces

In 1916, for the first time, women began to work in the armed services. At first they were used as volunteers in the Voluntary Aid Detachments (VADs), where they worked behind the lines as nurses (see Source G).

Much more important was the fact that, from early 1917, women began to be recruited as full-time members of the armed forces. The Women's Auxiliary Army Corps (WAAC) was set up in January 1917. They took over many of the office jobs in the army, which freed the men to fight. The Women's Royal Naval Service (WRNS) and the Women's Royal Air Force (WRAF) were set up in 1917 and 1918 respectively.

SOURCE G

Looking back on my time as a VAD in hospital, I think that it was the happiest time I ever spent, for it was all so worthwhile. The men who suffered did so because of their terrible heroism, not just because they had pneumonia or had been run over in the street. And no matter how tired one was, what horrible things one had to do, it was worthwhile to work until one could work no longer.

One woman's description of her time in the VAD in a book written after the First World War.

SOURCE H

▲ **Women air mechanics of the Women's Royal Air Force, established in 1918.**

The role of Lloyd George

Lloyd George as Minister for Munitions

The 'Great Shell Shortage' of 1915 (see page 18) had profound and far-reaching effects upon both the war and the country. The most immediate effect was the creation of a new ministry, the Ministry of Munitions. The new minister was David Lloyd George. He became responsible for reorganising the munitions industry on a real war footing.

Until May 1915 Lloyd George had been Chancellor of the Exchequer, a post that he had held since 1908. Lloyd George was a fiery and determined character who had played a major role in the Liberal reforms before the First World War. He had also been the leading figure in the struggle between the Liberals and the Conservative majority in the House of Lords during the years from 1909 to 1911.

Lloyd George's impact on the munitions industry was dramatic. Until May 1915 each battalion had been allotted four machine guns. Lloyd George increased the number to 64. He also increased the number of factories producing guns and ammunition for the armed forces. To ensure that supplies of raw materials were forthcoming, Lloyd George also brought quarries, mines, and many private firms, under government control. Businessmen were brought in to run the new munitions industry.

The Ministry of Munitions also took over the development of the tank (it had previously been in the hands of the Admiralty). Until 1915 there had been little interest in the tank from either the army or the War Ministry. Under Lloyd George it was developed into a practical weapon, although it proved of little use until 1917 at the Battle of Cambrai, as the tanks kept breaking down or got stuck in the mud. Lloyd George's changes ensured that there were no further problems with the supply of weapons and ammunition.

Lloyd George as Secretary of State for War

There was a turning point in the war in June 1916 when Lloyd George became Secretary of State for War (after the death of Lord Kitchener). He now demanded complete control of war policy. For the remainder of the war he also had a series of disagreements with Field Marshal Haig, who he believed was wasting lives on the Western Front. Lloyd George wanted to step up the war effort and make defeating Germany the number one priority. Eventually this led to a rift with the prime minister, Herbert Asquith, in November 1916. Asquith resigned at the beginning of December and Lloyd George replaced him as prime minister.

SOURCE A

▲ David Lloyd George.

Lloyd George as prime minister

Lloyd George's first and probably most significant act was to set up a War Cabinet of just five ministers, who met daily to deal with the war. This was a coalition government. In addition to Lloyd George (a Liberal) there were three Conservatives – Curzon, Milner and Balfour – and Henderson, who was Labour. Winning the war was their number one priority.

War Socialism

In 1917 Lloyd George introduced his policy of 'War Socialism': the taking of firm government control of the resources of the country.

■ The **railway** network was taken over so that transport could be co-ordinated more effectively. In 1914 there had been more than 120 different railway companies. In 1917 a unified system was created for the first time, which enabled troops and war materials to be moved around Britain far more efficiently.

■ All **coalmines** were taken over. In 1917 coal was the most important fuel: it not only heated most homes, but was also needed to produce iron and steel, and to provide the power for trains and most ships. War Socialism was very successful and in 1917 production reached an all-time record of 262 million tonnes. At the same time wages in the industry rose and the safety record improved.

■ **Shipyards** were also taken over and all British **merchant ships** were requisitioned (formally handed over). These actions were an attempt to replace the losses of merchant ships from German attacks and to increase the size of the Royal Navy. In 1916 the German Navy had begun unrestricted submarine warfare, which meant that ships sailing to British ports were sunk on sight. This was an attempt to starve Britain into surrendering by sinking merchant ships in the Atlantic. In the first half of 1917 the Germans had sunk 800,000 tonnes of British shipping.

In response to the attacks, Lloyd George ordered merchant ships to sail in **convoys** for protection and forced the Royal Navy to provide escorts. The Admiralty did not want its warships used as protection for slow moving merchant ships. However, Lloyd George forced the Admiralty to agree, and from October 1917 the number of ships sunk by German U-boats fell. Nevertheless, during the war about one-third of all British merchant ships were sunk.

■ **Food production** was also taken over during War Socialism. This gave the government the power to control what food was being produced. This had become very important as a result of submarine attacks. In 1914 Britain only produced about 60 per cent of its food supply, but by 1918 this had been increased to more than 90 per cent.

■ The **Ministry of Labour** was set up, which was responsible for organising the nation's labour force. It also introduced Directed Labour, which gave the government the power to force skilled workers to remain in occupations of national importance. This was an unpopular move with trade unions, as it curtailed a worker's right to change his job. In 1917 there was a series of strikes in protest against Directed Labour, especially in shipyards.

Lloyd George also created the **Ministry of Information**, headed by Lord Beaverbrook, the owner of the *Daily Express*. This ministry was used to influence foreign governments and neutral countries through propaganda. It printed pamphlets and also produced propaganda films.

Rationing

Despite the creation of the Ministry of Food Production and the introduction of the convoy system, food supplies began to run short in 1917.

The Defence of the Realm Act (see page 9) had given the government the power to start rationing food, but nothing was done until late 1917, when food shortages began to appear for the first time. The most important problem was the price of bread, which began to rise as wheat supplies from Canada and the USA were affected by the German U-boat campaign. In May 1917 'voluntary rationing' was introduced and the Royal Family announced that it was going to reduce consumption of bread by one quarter. In November 1917 the government began to control the price of bread and produced posters and recipe books encouraging people to be more careful with flour.

The real concern was that richer people would be able to afford higher prices, while working people would not. There had been strikes for higher pay during 1917 and the government had agreed to pay rises for industrial workers. By the end of the year the government was also subsidising the prices of bread and potatoes to try to ensure that everyone could afford basic foodstuffs.

Rationing was finally introduced in January 1918. The Ministry of Food supplied everyone with a National Ration Book. This contained coupons that were cut out by shopkeepers when food was bought. Also, everybody had to register with a shopkeeper for their supply of food. This involved a major effort on the part of the government, who needed to ensure that people received the food that they were entitled to, and that shopkeepers were supplied with the necessary stocks on a daily basis.

In fact, the main problem was not that stocks of food were low, but rather that people were beginning to hoard food, which meant that supplies were lower than they should have been. At first rationing only applied to meat, but in July 1918 sugar, butter, margarine and cooking fat were added. Food sold in restaurants was also controlled.

Sugar

Cheese

Wheat

Butter

Bacon

Fruit

0   25   50   75   100%

▲ **Percentages of food imported in 1913.**

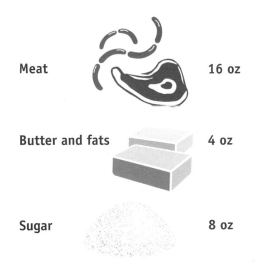

Meat — 16 oz

Butter and fats — 4 oz

Sugar — 8 oz

▲ **Rations per person per week in ounces in 1918.**

People who broke the rationing regulations could be punished severely. Stealing a ration book was punishable by three months in prison. A shopkeeper who supplied food illegally could be fined as much as £75, which was the equivalent of seven or eight months' wages for many working people.

The amounts allowed for people under the rationing regulations were generous, certainly by comparison with the Second World War, and there were no real shortages. However, there were queues outside some shops in February and March 1918 before food supplies from the spring and summer harvests became available.

In some cases, rationing actually had the effect of increasing food consumption, because most people bought their full rations, even if they did not actually need them or want them.

Most working people found that they were better fed by 1918 than they had been before the outbreak of war. There was also clear evidence in a number of reports that rationing had a beneficial effect on the health of children. In London and the other big cities, school medical inspections showed that the numbers of children suffering from malnutrition fell by 50 per cent. At the same time, the proportion of children who were allowed free school meals dropped during the years of the war.

Overall, Lloyd George's actions in 1917 and 1918 marked a complete change in government policy. This was the first time that the British government had assumed such responsibility for the people of Britain and for its economy. Lloyd George's policies were major factors in the winning of the war.

The Representation of the People Act, 1918

When the First World War broke out in 1914, women could not vote in general elections in Britain. In fact, not all men could vote either. In most cases men qualified to vote by the household franchise. This meant that they were entitled to vote if they had occupied a house for six months, or rented lodgings for twelve months.

Women had fought for the right to vote in the years leading up to the outbreak of war, but without success. The violent activities of the Suffragettes had persuaded many MPs to vote against giving women the vote, because they did not want to appear to be giving into violence. But the efforts of women on the Home Front changed many minds. For example, Herbert Asquith had always opposed votes for women, but in 1916 he admitted that

the war could not have been won without their efforts and that women had proved they were responsible enough to vote. But other factors also led to the extension of the franchise.

The right to vote

In 1915 a coalition government had been created. A second one was formed in 1916 when Lloyd George replaced Asquith as prime minister. In 1916 the government attempted to produce a new electoral register: a list of all the people in Britain who were entitled to vote. It was soon obvious that many men who had been entitled to vote in 1914 were now no longer qualified to vote. The reason was their service in the army, which meant that they had left home for France or elsewhere. If the old household franchise was retained, many millions of men who had fought 'for king and country' would lose their right to vote. This would have been a very serious issue, particularly as conscription had been introduced for the first time. It would have seemed very unfair if the government decided that it had the right to force men to fight and perhaps die for their country, but then said that they had no right to vote in elections. So the government decided not to tamper with the household franchise, but to create a completely new way of deciding who had the right to vote. The Representation of the People Act of 1918 granted the vote to all men aged 21 and over. The government even went so far as to put a temporary clause in the Act which allowed men over the age of eighteen to vote if they had served in the war.

Votes for women

While all men over 21 were being given the right to vote, the government also took the opportunity to give the vote to women. It could claim that it was rewarding women for proving their responsibility by their efforts during the war. By 1918 there were in fact few politicians who were prepared to argue against women's suffrage. When the vote was finally taken in the House of Commons in December 1917, there were 364 in favour and 23 against.

The Act did, however, have a sting in the tail. Women were not given the vote on equal terms with men in 1918. Although men were given the vote at the age of 21, women had to be aged 30 or over, and they also had to be householders or married to householders. The main reason for this was that Parliament did not want women voters to outnumber male voters. There was also the belief that women were still not as mature as men, and therefore needed to be older and show more responsibility before they could be entrusted with the vote.

While the Representation of the People Act allowed women to vote, it did not allow them to become MPs. However, in November 1918, just before the general election in December, the government rushed the Eligibility of Women Act through Parliament. This allowed women to stand as candidates in the general elections. In the event, only one woman was elected: Countess Markiewicz, who was elected for Sinn Fein in South Dublin. But along with the other 72 Sinn Fein MPs, she refused to recognise the legitimacy of the Westminster Parliament to legislate for Ireland, and she never took her seat. The sixteen other women who stood for Parliament in 1918 were all defeated. However, in 1919 Nancy Astor became the first woman to take her seat in the House of Commons.

The end of the war: 'A home fit for heroes'

The First World War came to an end at 11.00 am on the eleventh day of the eleventh month of 1918. People were overjoyed when they heard the news and there was an overwhelming belief that such a war should never take place again. Lloyd George spoke of a 'war to end all wars'.

People were also determined that something good should come out of the war. Lloyd George also spoke of a 'land fit for heroes to live in'. By this expression he meant that all those who had fought were heroes and that they should be treated as such when they returned to civilian life.

However, the war had cost a great deal of money and Britain owed the USA £850 million. At the same time, Britain had lent Russia £1750 million that was never repaid (because of the Russian revolution). There was a short post-war boom, as the British people celebrated victory, but after that the 1920s was a period of hardship.

UXBRIDGE LEARNING

How did the war change the role and status of women in Britain?

For most women, the end of the war was the end of their working life. Some had only intended to work for the duration of the war, as part of an attempt to support their men at the Front. But many gave up their jobs reluctantly, with regret at the loss of the freedom their jobs had brought them. The term 'Heroines to Scroungers' was used as moral blackmail, to persuade them to give up their jobs now that the war was over. Source A shows another method of persuasion.

 **SOURCE A**

I ask you, young lady, who are now able to wear expensive hats and gloves and shoes and stockings, to just stop for a minute – think of the hundreds of acres adorned with small wooden crosses; think of the agonies some of the bodies under the crosses endured. I am sure that giving up your job for one of those men who has done so much for you, will be more than enough reward.

Extract published in a magazine in October 1920 showing the methods used to encourage women to give up their jobs at the end of the war.

Even so, the end of the war saw a continued rise in women's employment. Within three years, the number of women working as domestic servants had risen to 1,845,000, well above its pre-war level.

Social changes

The war did, however, lead to real changes in social attitudes. Women now had more freedom and their clothing became much simpler, with shorter skirts and sleeves. Hairstyles changed and wearing trousers became more acceptable. Women also gained more control over their lives. In the 1920s contraception became available for the first time through the work of Marie Stopes. Few women were able to take advantage of this at first, but the social stigma of using contraception began to be reduced. Also, the medical, legal and teaching professions all began to accept women more readily. However, only in elementary education did women achieve dominance.

Legal changes

In addition to the right to vote, the years after the war saw a number of important Acts of Parliament passed that gave women significant legal rights. In 1919 the Sex Disqualification Act made discrimination against women in some professions illegal. In 1922 the Law of Property Act gave husbands and wives equal rights to inherit each other's property. In 1923 divorce became easier for women: they could now divorce their husbands on equal terms. Until 1923 a wife had had to prove two causes for divorce out of adultery, cruelty and desertion, while a man only had to prove one. In practice, however, these Acts had little immediate impact on the lives of women. Only the wealthy and socially privileged were able to take advantage of this new legislation. For many women the 1920s were little different from the 1910s.

Sample coursework assignment

When war broke out in 1914, most people in Britain expected that it would be over in a matter of months. Accordingly, the slogan of the government was 'business as usual'. Only gradually did the full horror begin to dawn, and with it, the mobilisation of the nation to win the war at all costs.

In this assignment you will investigate how the lives of people in Britain changed as a result of the war and try to discover how important the role of the Home Front was in the winning of the war.

SOURCE A

I was in domestic service and 'hated every minute of it' when the war broke out, earning £2 a month working from 6.00 am to 9.00 pm. So when the need came for women 'war-workers' my chance came to 'out'. I started on hand-cutting shell fuses. We worked twelve hours a day, apart from the journey morning and night. As for wages, I thought I was very well off earning £5 a week.

A letter written in 1976 by a woman who lived through the First World War.

SOURCE B

In July 1916 I was approached by women working at a London aircraft works. They were painting aircraft wings with dope varnish at a wage of 15 shillings a week, for which they had to work from 8 am to 5.30 pm. They were frequently expected to work on till 8 pm and were only paid normal rates for this overtime. It was common, they told me, for six or more of the thirty dope painters to be lying ill on the stones outside the workshop, for half an hour, or three-quarters, before being able to return to their toil.

Part of a book written by Sylvia Pankhurst in 1932.

SOURCE C

Typical cases which have come under my personal observation show that women prefer factory life. They like the freedom, the spirit of independence fostered by their new-found earning power, the social life. The children, they say, are better off than before, better fed, housed and clothed.

Part of a book written in 1917 by the owner of a factory in Birmingham.

SOURCE D

▲ A photograph taken in a munitions factory during the First World War. The words on the board at the back read 'When the boys come back we are not going to keep you any longer – girls'.

SOURCE E

THESE WOMEN ARE DOING THEIR BIT

LEARN TO MAKE MUNITIONS

▲ A poster produced by the British government in 1916.

SOURCE F

	1914	1918
Transport	18,200	117,200
Manufacturing industry	2,178,600	2,970,600
Domestic Service	1,658,000	1,258,000
Civil Servants and teachers	262,000	460,200

▲ Numbers of women employed in British industries in 1914 and 1918.

SOURCE G

Over and over again the foreman gave me the wrong or incomplete directions and altered them in such a way as to create hours more work. I had no tools that I needed, and it was only on Saturdays that I could get to a shop. It was out of the question to borrow anything from the men.

Two shop stewards informed me on the first day that they had no objection to my working there provided I received the full (men's) rate of pay. But after this none of the men spoke to me for a long time, and would give me no help as to where to find things. My drawer was nailed up by the men, and another night oil was poured over everything in it, through a crack.

Part of an account of one woman's experiences while working during the First World War; this was written in 1919.

SOURCE H

Women can satisfactorily handle much heavier pieces of metal than had been previously dreamt of.

Part of an article in *The Engineer,* published in August 1915.

SOURCE I

She has discarded her petticoats. There are girls at the wheels of half the cars that pass. If you go by train, women will handle your luggage. If you choose bus or tram, the conductress in her smart uniform has long been a familiar figure in our streets.

Part of a report on *Woman's work in wartime* published in 1918.

SOURCE J

▲ The painting 'For King and Country' by E. F. Skinner, 1917.

❓ Assignment One: Objective 1

1. Describe the employment opportunities for women in Britain in 1914 at the outbreak of the First World War. **(15)**

2. Why did the number of women employed in Britain begin to rise significantly from mid-1915? **(15)**

3. In what ways did the First World War change the employment opportunities for women in Britain? **(20)**

(Total: 50 marks)

❓ Assignment Two: Objectives 2 and 3

1. Study Source A. What can you learn from Source A about women's work during the First World War? **(6)**

2. Study Sources A, B and C. Does the evidence in Source C support the evidence in Sources A and B about women's work in the First World War? Explain your answer. **(8)**

3. Study Sources D and E. How useful are Sources D and E in helping you to understand the importance of the work of women in industry during the First World War? **(10)**

4. Study Source G. Use Source G and your own knowledge to explain why some men opposed the employment of women in industry during the First World War. **(12)**

5. Study all the sources.

   'Without the work of women on the Home Front, Britain could not have won the First World War.'

   Use the sources and your own knowledge to explain whether you agree with this view. **(14)**

(Total: 50 marks)